BROADWAY ★ 20 PIANO SOLOS

ISBN 978-1-70512-174-0

HAL•LEONARD®

Visit Hal Leonard Online at
www.halleonard.com

Contact us:
Hal Leonard
7777 West Bluemound Road
Milwaukee, WI 53213
Email: info@halleonard.com

In Europe, contact:
Hal Leonard Europe Limited
42 Wigmore Street
Marylebone, London, W1U 2RN
Email: info@halleonardeurope.com

In Australia, contact:
Hal Leonard Australia Pty. Ltd.
4 Lentara Court
Cheltenham, Victoria, 3192 Australia
Email: info@halleonard.com.au

ALL I ASK OF YOU
from THE PHANTOM OF THE OPERA

Music by ANDREW LLOYD WEBBER
Lyrics by CHARLES HART
Additional Lyrics by RICHARD STILGOE

Andante

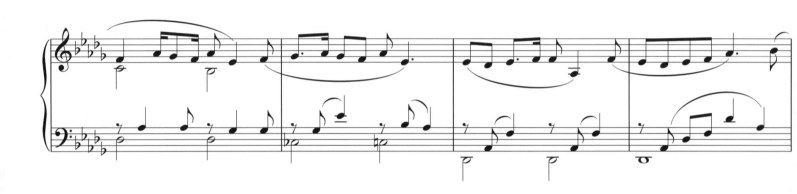

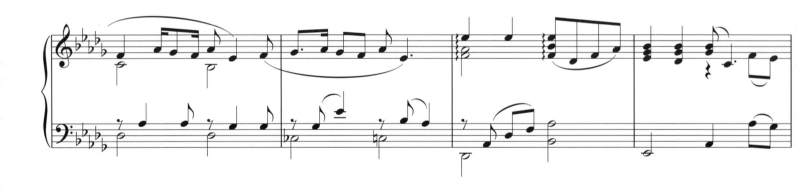

ANSWER ME
from THE BAND'S VISIT

Words and Music by
DAVID YAZBEK

Slowly, in 2

Add cues 2nd time

6

BURN
from HAMILTON

Words and Music by
LIN-MANUEL MIRANDA

CONSIDER YOURSELF
from the Broadway Musical OLIVER!

Words and Music by
LIONEL BART

DO I LOVE YOU BECAUSE YOU'RE BEAUTIFUL

from CINDERELLA

Lyrics by OSCAR HAMMERSTEIN II
Music by RICHARD RODGERS

GETTING TO KNOW YOU

from THE KING AND I

Lyrics by OSCAR HAMMERSTEIN II
Music by RICHARD RODGERS

Gracefully

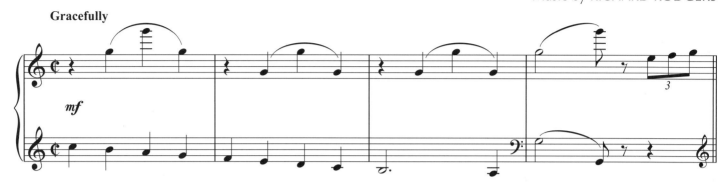

ON MY OWN
from LES MISÉRABLES

Music by CLAUDE-MICHEL SCHÖNBERG
Lyrics by ALAIN BOUBLIL, JEAN-MARC NATEL,
HERBERT KRETZMER, JOHN CAIRD
and TREVOR NUNN

IF I LOVED YOU

from CAROUSEL

Lyrics by OSCAR HAMMERSTEIN II
Music by RICHARD RODGERS

Moderately slow

MAKE SOMEONE HAPPY

from DO RE MI

Words by BETTY COMDEN and ADOLPH GREEN
Music by JULE STYNE

MEMORY
from CATS

Music by ANDREW LLOYD WEBBER
Text by TREVOR NUNN after T.S. ELIOT

Freely and expressively

OVER THE RAINBOW
from THE WIZARD OF OZ

Music by HAROLD ARLEN
Lyric by E.Y. "YIP" HARBURG

SUMMER NIGHTS

from GREASE

Lyric and Music by WARREN CASEY
and JIM JACOBS

8vb

PEOPLE WILL SAY WE'RE IN LOVE

from OKLAHOMA!

Lyrics by OSCAR HAMMERSTEIN II
Music by RICHARD RODGERS

Moderately, in 2

With motion

THIS IS THE MOMENT

from JEKYLL & HYDE

Words and Music by LESLIE BRICUSSE
and FRANK WILDHORN

44

TOMORROW
from the Musical Production ANNIE

Lyric by MARTIN CHARNIN
Music by CHARLES STROUSE

TRY TO REMEMBER

from THE FANTASTICKS

Words by TOM JONES
Music by HARVEY SCHMIDT

UNUSUAL WAY
from NINE

Music and Lyrics by
MAURY YESTON

WISHING YOU WERE SOMEHOW HERE AGAIN

from THE PHANTOM OF THE OPERA

Music by ANDREW LLOYD WEBBER
Lyrics by CHARLES HART
Additional Lyrics by RICHARD STILGOE

Slightly faster

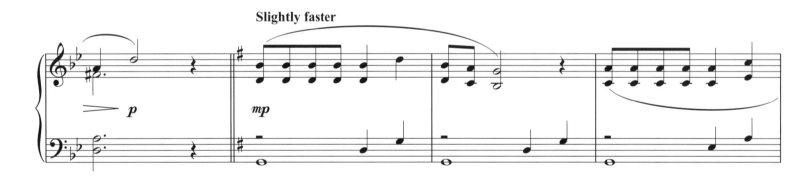

WITH YOU
from PIPPIN

Words and Music by
STEPHEN SCHWARTZ

A WONDERFUL DAY LIKE TODAY

from THE ROAR OF THE GREASEPAINT—THE SMELL OF THE CROWD

Words and Music by LESLIE BRICUSSE
and ANTHONY NEWLEY

YOUR FAVORITE MUSIC
ARRANGED FOR PIANO SOLO

ADELE FOR PIANO SOLO – 2ND EDITION
This collection features 13 Adele favorites beautifully arranged for piano solo, including: Chasing Pavements • Hello • Rolling in the Deep • Set Fire to the Rain • Someone like You • Turning Tables • When We Were Young • and more.
00307585 ....$14.99

PRIDE & PREJUDICE
12 piano pieces from the 2006 Oscar-nominated film, including: Another Dance • Darcy's Letter • Georgiana • Leaving Netherfield • Liz on Top of the World • Meryton Townhall • The Secret Life of Daydreams • Stars and Butterflies • and more.
00313327 ....$17.99

BATTLESTAR GALACTICA
by Bear McCreary
For this special collection, McCreary himself has translated the acclaimed orchestral score into fantastic solo piano arrangements at the intermediate to advanced level. Includes 19 selections in all, and as a bonus, simplified versions of "Roslin and Adama" and "Wander My Friends." Contains a note from McCreary, as well as a biography.
00313530 ....$17.99

GEORGE GERSHWIN – RHAPSODY IN BLUE (ORIGINAL)
Alfred Publishing Co.
George Gershwin's own piano solo arrangement of his classic contemporary masterpiece for piano and orchestra. This masterful measure-for-measure two-hand adaptation of the complete modern concerto for piano and orchestra incorporates all orchestral parts and piano passages into two staves while retaining the clarity, sonority, and brilliance of the original.
00321589 ....$16.99

THE BEST JAZZ PIANO SOLOS EVER
Over 300 pages of beautiful classic jazz piano solos featuring standards in any jazz artist's repertoire. Includes: Afternoon in Paris • Giant Steps • Moonlight in Vermont • Moten Swing • A Night in Tunisia • Night Train • On Green Dolphin Street • Song for My Father • West Coast Blues • Yardbird Suite • and more.
00312079 ....$19.99

ROMANTIC FILM MUSIC
40 piano solo arrangements of beloved songs from the silver screen, including: Anyone at All • Come What May • Glory of Love • I See the Light • I Will Always Love You • Iris • It Had to Be You • Nobody Does It Better • She • Take My Breath Away (Love Theme) • A Thousand Years • Up Where We Belong • When You Love Someone • The Wind Beneath My Wings • and many more.
00122112 ....$17.99

CLASSICS WITH A TOUCH OF JAZZ
Arranged by Lee Evans
27 classical masterpieces arranged in a unique and accessible jazz style. Mr Evans also provides an audio recording of each piece. Titles include: Air from Suite No. 3 (Bach) • Barcarolle "June" (Tchaikovsky) • Pavane (Faure) • Piano Sonata No. 8 "Pathetique" (Beethoven) • Reverie (Debussy) • The Swan (Saint-Saens) • and more.
00151662 Book/Online Audio..$14.99

STAR WARS: THE FORCE AWAKENS
Music from the soundtrack to the seventh installment of the Star Wars® franchise by John Williams is presented in this songbook, complete with artwork from the film throughout the whole book, including eight pages in full color! Titles include: The Scavenger • Rey Meets BB-8 • Rey's Theme • That Girl with the Staff • Finn's Confession • The Starkiller • March of the Resistance • Torn Apart • and more.
00154451 ....$17.99

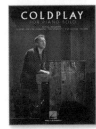

COLDPLAY FOR PIANO SOLO
Stellar solo arrangements of a dozen smash hits from Coldplay: Clocks • Fix You • In My Place • Lost! • Paradise • The Scientist • Speed of Sound • Trouble • Up in Flames • Viva La Vida • What If • Yellow.
00307637 ....$15.99

TAYLOR SWIFT FOR PIANO SOLO – 2ND EDITION
This updated second edition features 15 of Taylor's biggest hits from her self-titled first album all the way through her pop breakthrough album, *1989*. Includes: Back to December • Blank Space • Fifteen • I Knew You Were Trouble • Love Story • Mean • Mine • Picture to Burn • Shake It Off • Teardrops on My Guitar • 22 • We Are Never Ever Getting Back Together • White Horse • Wildest Dreams • You Belong with Me.
00307375 ....$16.99

DISNEY SONGS
12 Disney favorites in beautiful piano solo arrangements, including: Bella Notte (This Is the Night) • Can I Have This Dance • Feed the Birds • He's a Tramp • I'm Late • The Medallion Calls • Once Upon a Dream • A Spoonful of Sugar • That's How You Know • We're All in This Together • You Are the Music in Me • You'll Be in My Heart (Pop Version).
00313527 ....$14.99

UP
Music by Michael Giacchino
Piano solo arrangements of 13 pieces from Pixar's mammoth animated hit: Carl Goes Up • It's Just a House • Kevin Beak'n • Married Life • Memories Can Weigh You Down • The Nickel Tour • Paradise Found • The Small Mailman Returns • The Spirit of Adventure • Stuff We Did • We're in the Club Now • and more, plus a special section of full-color artwork from the film!
00313471 ....$17.99

GREAT THEMES FOR PIANO SOLO
Nearly 30 rich arrangements of popular themes from movies and TV shows, including: Bella's Lullaby • Chariots of Fire • Cinema Paradiso • The Godfather (Love Theme) • Hawaii Five-O Theme • Theme from "Jaws" • Theme from "Jurassic Park" • Linus and Lucy • The Pink Panther • Twilight Zone Main Title • and more.
00312102 ....$14.99

HAL•LEONARD®
7777 W. BLUEMOUND RD. P.O. BOX 13819 MILWAUKEE, WI 53213
www.halleonard.com

HAL LEONARD:
Your Source for the Best of Broadway

BEST BROADWAY SHEET MUSIC

80 songs: And All That Jazz • Bewitched, Bothered, and Bewildered • Corner of the Sky • Don't Rain on My Parade • Ease on Down the Road • Get Happy • Hernando's Hideaway • I Could Have Danced All Night • The Lady Is a Tramp • Mama Who Bore Me • On the Street Where You Live • People • Superboy and the Invisible Girl • This Is the Moment • Where or When • You Took Advantage of Me • and more.

00322453 Piano/Vocal/Guitar....................................$24.99

THE BEST BROADWAY SONGS EVER

85 timeless Broadway favorites: Bring Him Home • Cabaret • I Could Have Danced All Night • Memory • My Favorite Things • On the Street Where You Live • One • Popular • Somewhere • Sunrise, Sunset • Try to Remember • Waving Through a Window • You'll Never Walk Alone • and more.

00291992 Piano/Vocal/Guitar....................................$24.99

THE BIG BOOK OF BROADWAY

70 Broadway favorites from contemporary shows, including: *Annie, The Book of Mormon, Bye Bye Birdie, A Chorus Line, Guys and Dolls, Hairspray, Hello Dolly!, The King and I, Les Misérables, The Lion King, Mamma Mia!, Oklahoma!, Once, The Phantom of the Opera, The Producers, Rent, Singin' in the Rain, South Pacific,* and more.

00311658 Piano/Vocal/Guitar....................................$22.99

BROADWAY SHEET MUSIC COLLECTION: 2010-2017

39 favorites from contemporary Broadway hit shows – includes songs from: *The Addams Family, Aladdin, The Book of Mormon, Bright Star, A Bronx Tale, Come from Away, Dear Evan Hansen, Hamilton, Kinky Boots, Natasha Pierre and the Great Comet of 1812, Newsies, Something Rotten!, Waitress,* and more.

00248693 Piano/Vocal/Guitar....................................$24.95

BROADWAY SONGS

Get more bang for your buck with 73 songs from 56 shows, including *Annie Get Your Gun, Cabaret, The Full Monty, Jekyll & Hyde, Les Misérables, Oklahoma* and more. Songs: Any Dream Will Do • Consider Yourself • Footloose • Getting to Know You • I Dreamed a Dream • One • People • Summer Nights • The Surrey with the Fringe on Top • With One Look • and more.

00310832 Piano/Vocal/Guitar....................................$14.99

DEFINITIVE BROADWAY

120 Broadway classics, revised to include songs from the latest blockbusters as well as iconic classics such as: *Cabaret, Chicago, Evita, Gypsy, Mamma Mia!, Oklahoma!, The Phantom of the Opera, The Producers, The Sound of Music, Wicked,* and many more

00359570 Piano/Vocal/Guitar....................................$27.50

DISNEY ON BROADWAY

26 songs from nine Disney movie musicals: If I Can't Love Her (from *Beauty and the Beast*) • One Step Closer (from *The Little Mermaid*) • Proud of Your Boy (from *Aladdin*) • They Live in You (from *The Lion King*) • True Love (from *Frozen*) • Watch What Happens (from *Newsies*) • Written in the Stars (from *Aïda*) • and more.

00282444 Piano/Vocal/Guitar....................................$19.95

50 BROADWAY SHOWS/ 50 BROADWAY SONGS

Includes: Any Dream Will Do • Day by Day • Hello, Young Lovers • I Don't Know How to Love Him • I Dreamed a Dream • Oh! What a Beautiful Mornin' • Ol' Man River • Memory • Popular • Seasons of Love • Sunrise, Sunset • 'Til Him • What I Did for Love • You'll Never Walk Alone • and more!

00359867 Piano/Vocal/Guitar..........................$16.95

GREAT AMERICAN SONGBOOK: BROADWAY

100 timeless hits from the Great White Way: And All That Jazz • Beauty and the Beast • Don't Rain on My Parade • Edelweiss • Footloose • The Impossible Dream (The Quest) • Luck Be a Lady • Maria • New York, New York • One • Popular • Seasons of Love • The Surrey with the Fringe on Top • Tomorrow • You're the Top • and more.

00233276 Piano/Vocal/Guitar.....................$27.99

THE LIBRARY OF SHOWTUNES

Over 60 favorites: Big Spender • Close Every Door • Consider Yourself • Defying Gravity • Don't Cry for Me Argentina • I Dreamed a Dream • If I Were a Rich Man • Love Changes Everything • Luck Be a Lady • The Music of the Night • My Favorite Things • Oh, What a Beautiful Mornin' • On My Own • One • Singin' in the Rain • Suddenly Seymour • and more.

14042130 Piano/Vocal/Guitar.....................$19.99

LOVE SONGS FROM BROADWAY

Over 30 stunning love songs from your favorite Broadway musicals! Includes: All I Ask of You • Can You Feel the Love Tonight • Just the Way You Are • The Last Night of the World • Seasons of Love • She's Got a Way • Unexpected Song • Without Love • and dozens more.

00311474 Piano/Vocal/Guitar.....................$14.95

THE OFF-BROADWAY SONGBOOK

50 gems from off-Broadway hits, including *Altar Boyz; The Fantasticks; Floyd Collins; I Love You, You're Perfect, Now Change; The It Girl; Johnny Guitar; The Last Five Years; Myths and Hymns; Songs for a New World; tick tick...Boom!; [title of show]: The Wild Party;* and many more..

00311168 Piano/Vocal/Guitar.....................$19.99

PIANO BROADWAY HITS FOR DUMMIES

47 of Broadway's biggest songs: All I Ask of You (from *The Phantom of the Opera*) • Bring Him Home (from *Les Miserables*) • Defying Gravity (from *Wicked*) • Edelweiss (from *The Sound of Music*) • Memory (from *Cats*) • Ol' Man River (from *Showboat*) • Seasons of Love (from *Rent*) • Waving Through a Window (from *Dear Evan Hansen*) • and more.

00298820 Piano/Vocal/Guitar.....................$19.99

HAL•LEONARD®

Get complete songlists and order from your favorite music retailer at
halleonard.com